OBSERVATIONS ON THE PRINCIPLES AND METHODS
of
INFANT INSTRUCTION.

by Amos B. Alcott,
Teacher of an Elementary School, Boston.

Originally Printed in 1830.

© 1830, 2009 Seven Suns Distribution.
All rights reserved.

INFANT INSTRUCTION.

The tendency of the public mind, arising from the comparatively free spirit of our institutions in this country, towards the study and improvement of human nature, constitutes a feature of the present day, interesting in the highest degree to the Christian philosopher and philanthropist. The study of man is, of all others, a study of the first and highest importance. Character, natural and acquired, modified by temperament, by education, by society, government, and religion, is a subject worthy of all attention and analysis. All that affects its formation and its reformation; all that mysterious process by which the human mind accomplishes its great purposes—the perfecting of its nature, and the elevation of its hopes, should be regarded with a deep and scrutinizing attention, by all those entrusted with its high capacities and lofty destinies. To the teacher, the guardian, and the friend of man, all subjects involving in any degree his welfare, his improvement, and his happiness, present their claims for unbiassed inquiry and deep-felt interest.

Of the many methods, by which the wise and good of the present day, are contributing to the best interests of the mind, redeeming it from the slavery of ignorance and vice, to the liberty of intelligence, virtue, and happiness, the institutions of Infant Schools, now so generally established among us, are full of much promise and hope. Their present and increasing popularity; the amount of misery and vice which they relieve and prevent; the happiness and virtue which they create and encourage; their reception of children from all classes of society, at an age when every impression so much determines their future habits, motives, principles, and whole character, places them among the wisest and happiest agents of Christian beneficence. Cooperating with the influences of the nursery, in the formation of infant character, their benefits must be as great, as their principles are correct, and their methods successful.

The early influences operating upon infancy, embrace a variety of subjects, principles, and methods. Early education, involving the expansion, direction, and perfecting of the faculties of infant nature, is a subject wide and intricate. All the elements of this nature are embraced as its objects; in its principles and methods a discipline is required, adapted to the order in which these faculties appear, to their relative importance as aids in life, and to their gradual and harmonious developement by a wise selection of exercises and means. The animal nature, the affections, the conscience, and the intellect, present their united claims for distinct and systematic attention. The whole being of the child asks for expansion and guidance. In the constitution of his nature, shall we, therefore, find the principles of infant cultivation.

If we observe the habits of infancy in a physiological point view of view, its active propensities cannot fail to meet our notice. The child is essentially an active being. His chief enjoyment consists in the free and natural exercise of his material frame. The quickening instinct of his nature urges him to the exertion of all its functions and to seek in this, every means for their varied and happy activity. A reverential respect for the author of so benevoler a law of its animal economy, will suggest a faithful obedience to its requisitions. The claims of animal nature in infancy, are primary and paramount to all others; and it is not till these are anticipated and relieved by unrestrained movement, that the intellect can be successfully addressed. By encouraging the free and natural activity of the body, the functions on which intellectual energy and happiness depend, are invigorated and most effectually prepared for the lessons of instruction. Play is the appointed dispensation of childhood; and a beneficent wisdom consists in turning this to its designed purpose. When the force of animal impulse has expended itself by free and natural recreation, and left the physical system in a state of tranquillity, the mind imbibes the influence, and forgetting the scenes and activities of its previous joys, yields itself to the loftier claims of its nature, and asks the sympathy and guidance of instruction; and it is by creating, and applying these states of the animal and intellectual nature, for the advancement of the child, that successful results are chiefly produced in early instruction.

The primary want of infancy is enjoyment. In seeking to supply this want from the variety of surrounding objects, the child often fails of his purpose, from the want of reflection and experience. His mind thus becomes saddened by disappointment, his temper impaired, his reason sophisticated and weakened. He needs the hand of friendly guidance and aid. The means employed by the infant system, should guide him to the true and lasting sources of enjoyment. Respecting all the laws of his animal economy, they should associate pleasure with the action of all his faculties, investing all his instructions with an interest, a certainty, and a love, which future experience shall not diminish, nor maturer reason disapprove. By yielding a more intelligent homage to the active propensities of infancy, furnishing a greater proportion, and a more intellectual kind of recreation, than is permitted by other forms of discipline, the infant system diffuses over the young mind the benign and improving influences of happiness, and thus imparts intellectual and moral life to the infant spirit.

The provision which is thus made for the exercise of the animal functions, extends its influence beyond their developement, to the affectionate nature of the child. Associating with minds like his own in the common purposes of amusement and happiness, his affections find free and spontaneous action to multiply and elevate the joys of his existence, to connect him in ties of sympathy and love with his infant friends, and thus to unseal within him the fountains of future felicity. By multiplying and purifying the sensations of his nature, an experienced wisdom is acquired by the child, which, under more restrained and unsocial influences, it would be impossible to impart. A play-room thus becomes an important aid both to intellectual improvement and happiness. An attentive instructer will see in its amusements the true results of his labors; for it is in the freedom of these, that infant character is most clearly revealed. As in the theatre of adult life, we learn the true characters of men by friendly intercommunication, and frequent collision of purposes and interests; so in the amusements of the play-room, the arena of infant activity and impulse, will a wise instructer obtain a just knowledge of infant character. Instruction, unless connected with active duty, and expressed in character, can be at best but a doubtful good. For the improvement of the animal and the affectionate nature, the play-room thus becomes an indispensable appendage to the Infant School. In its unpremeditated sports, and under careful superintendence, without restraint or interdiction, except in cases of obvious wrong, the child is happily employed, and most effectually prepared for the more formal lessons of the school-room.

In the general culture resulting from the play-room, it would be as unwise as impracticable to attempt systematic exercises, or descend into positive detail. It is in the school-room that the faculties of infancy are to be separately addressed, and that systematic attention becomes a necessary requisite. And in proceeding to more systematic labors, the intelligent teacher will seek, as before, his chief guidance in the principles pervading the intellectual and moral constitution of the child. By these will he shape out his system, and on these will he raise the fabric of infant character.

The affections will claim his first attention. On the cultivation and direction of these, much of infant happiness depends. A beneficent wisdom will not fail to discern in their early strength and prominence, the obvious intentions of nature, and yield a religious obedience to her unerring requisitions. Affectionate and familiar conversation is the chief avenue to the infant mind. This will invariably reach its recesses, and reflect its influences, in corresponding tones and emotions. This is the powerful spring which puts the young heart in action, and unfolds all its faculties in the sweetest harmony and perfection. What only is felt by the teacher can become effectual in its purpose, or happy in its influence upon the taught; for all truly efficient results must come from the heart.

In an institution so purely moral in its purpose as the Infant School, much depends upon the character of the teacher. Moral results can come only from moral means; and of these the teachers agency is the chief. In him the infant mind should find the object of its imitation and its love. To a pure and affectionate heart, an unsophisticated conscience, and elevated principles of action, the teacher should unite an amiableness of temper, a simplicity of manner, and a devotion to his work, which shall associate with it his happiness and his duty. His mind should be well disciplined by various experience; beautified and adorned by the cultivation of its moral attributes, and purified and elevated by the faith and hopes of Christianity. To these should be added, as an indispensable requisite, a familiar acquaintance with the infant mind, and a deep reverence for its author. He should possess the power of reaching the infant understanding in the simplest and happiest forms; of investing truth in the loveliest attributes, associating liberty and delight with all the means of its pursuit. Free from prejudices and partialities, he should impart instructions from the pure fountains of truth and love alone. Taking a benevolent view of the works of nature and the ways of Providence, his piety should diffuse itself through all his teachings, and with a silent, quickening power, draw wisdom and improvement from every event. Of mere learning he may have little or much; an intelligent philanthropy, a desire to be useful, are more important requisites, and without which his other attainments will be of little avail. Of patience and self-control, he should be a thorough and constant disciple.

Intimately connected with the cultivation of the affections, is the diviner nature of the child; the conscience. This fundamental principle of all virtue early reveals itself as a subject of attention and culture. To train and elevate this by frequent appeals to the unerring laws of reason, rectitude, and benevolence, is an all-important work. It is on this portion of infant nature, that the purest influences should fall, and from which the noblest results should be anticipated. Conscientiousness is the parent of all the noblest virtues, and forms the primary attribute of a pure and lofty character. It is by its wise and happy cultivation that the infant mind finds within, the sources of self-dependence, and self-control, and by its divine suggestions is led to the knowledge and worship of its author, and to the divine truths of the Christian revelation. An unrelaxing attention should, therefore, be given to all instruction that affects motive, since it is this which lays the permanent foundations of character, and constitutes the true glory of the soul.

The union of these influences, operating upon the animal, the affectionate, and the spiritual nature, like the quickening and expanding airs of spring upon the material world, reaches the intellectual portion of the child, and prepares the way for direct intellectual culture. Every mental faculty should be effectually addressed, and be made to operate in the independent acquisition of knowledge. Formal precepts, abstract reasonings, and unintelligible instructions, should here find no place; but interesting incidents, familiar descriptions, approaching as nearly as possible to the circumstances and relations of life, should embody no inconsiderable portion of the lessons of infancy. All that connects the child with the pure, the good, and the happy around him, should be impressed deeply in his mind. From the opened volume of nature, always perused with delight by childhood; from the varied records of life and experience, and from the deeper fountains of the mind, and of revelation, illustrations of truth and love may be drawn to expand the infant soul, to elevate and enrich it with knowledge and piety, for the coming years of its existence. Truth alone, in its divine unity and beauty, should be presented.

All lessons should reach the mind in an intelligible and visible form. In this way alone can they find a response in the heart, operate in conscience, and impart energy and life to knowledge and duty.

The work of the infant teacher, simple and attainable as it may seem, involves, however, in its methods and details, resources of the purest and happiest character; imposes responsibilities of the deepest kind. But these considerations will never deter the true friend of infancy, from the prosecution of his work. In the simple desire to bless, in the consciousness that of all others, his are labors of usefulness and love, dwells both the principle and the means, that shall lead him in time to reward and success. Patience and experience will become his sure and confiding friends. Acquainted with the constitution of the infant mind, and knowing that immediate and apparent results are not to come from his labors, his anxiety will not prematurely hasten their approach. The mind, he knows, is not to be perfected in a day; nor is truth to reach it, and stamp its permanent impression; nor character attain its symmetry, and reveal its strength and perfection, at once. These are the slow product of time and labor: they are the united results of nature and art: they come from providence and instruction. It is the imperceptible and gentle influence of the dews of heaven that gradually expands the opening flower into all its beauty, fragrance and perfection; and so must it be with the opening mind of infancy. And much early labor will consist in shielding this from noxious influences, ere habit, and conscience, and principle have reached their full strength and activity. A religious reverence for the infant mind as the image of its author, will not wantonly pervert its powers by premature temptation, dim its joys by the regrets of disappointment, nor corrode its nature by the restraints of distrust and fear. Infant happiness should be but another name for infant progress; nature, and providence, and instruction, cooperating in their influences to elevate and to bless the infant spirit.

The methods by which the principles and purposes of early culture are applied in the exercise of the school-room, are of the most simple and unpretending character. They preserve all the primary habits of infancy, as expressed in the nursery, and under the observation and affection of a judicious and devoted mother at home. Instruction drawn from common circumstances and objects, assumes all the freedom and simplicity of domestic conversation; and so far as consistent with common order and discipline, follows the unpremeditated thoughts and feelings of every child. The teacher comes as much in direct contact with each as he can; avoiding all general instructions, except for the purpose of mental relaxation, or of improving the faculties of sympathy, and imitation. Much systematic instruction is repulsive to the habits and feelings of infancy. Order and system, when carried into minute detail, often become to the child, but other names for restraint and unhappiness, and whatever associates these with the operations of the mind, or the impulses of duty, claims no place among early influences. The more direct, therefore, and individual the methods of instruction become in their influence, the more efficient and happy will be their results. The growth and energy of the mind depend upon the freedom and happiness of its movements, and the restraints imposed by system for its action with others, cannot essentially conduce to its benefit. Instruction should refer to the circumstances of coming life and duty. In these, general movements are seldom required. It is through individual channels that the purest and most efficient influences reach the mind, and from this, connect themselves, in the same way, with duty and improvement.

There is no attainment of the teacher more difficult to possess, and at the same time more indispensable, than the power of making himself understood; of conversing intelligibly with children. The range of the infant mind is comparatively confined; all its operations are within a narrow circle. With the fleeting and varied impressions made by the objects within this circle upon its perceptive power, through the medium of the senses, it is the work of the instructer to become acquainted, and to give the image of permanence and truth, by the terms of language. And he is besides this to bring up from the fountains of love and thought, the more refined and evanescent objects within, and give them their true expression and beauty. The language of the teacher, and all his methods of intellectual communion, to be intelligent, must, therefore, descend to the scanty vocabulary of infant thought, drawn from the circle of its observation and experience. It must find a response and an interpreter within, or to the infant ear, he utters instructions in an unknown tongue, and converses only with himself. From whatever source the lessons of the infant school are drawn, the truths they contain should be invested in the simplest and purest forms of language, and associated with nature and happiness. Early impressions, whether true or false, derive their chief power over the mind, and exert their influence upon life and happiness, through association; and this is the result of education. How important is it therefore in infant instruction, that the distinctions between truth and error, should be religiously preserved, and correctly associated with intelligence and duty. Of this associating power, language is the chief instrument to be used; the connecting link between material and intellectual nature; the channel through which thought and feeling, truth and love, are to pass between the teacher and the child. Let him be careful of perverting this power. Let him be sure that he well understands what he presents to their minds; and that they understand what he presents: for in all misapprehension on the part of either, there is perversion, there is error; and who shall answer for the consequence! There is no principle in infant instruction, in yielding obedience to which, the responsibility and the success of the teacher, are more involved than in this.

In seeking the primary methods indicated by nature for the instruction of infancy, the faithful observer will recognise in the universal fondness of children for stories and pictures, a ready and happy means of influence. From these no inconsiderable portion of their lessons may be drawn. Next to the free and natural expansion of their powers in play, in the observation of nature and of life, the story and the picture offer them the greatest charms; and by addressing all their moral and intellectual sympathies, contribute most effectually to their culture. To them the story is intellectual play. It is amusement in which their own enjoyments, their pleasures and their pains, are continued and represented in the persons of others. Their willing attention is consequently secured. The incidents, the thoughts, and the feelings thus drawn from subjects so interesting and familiar to their minds, and presented in the simplest tones and language of affection, cannot but delight them. When embodying the purest attributes of truth, connecting motive and principle with action, the story thus becomes a ready channel for moral instruction to reach the mind. Virtue, wisdom, and goodness, in this way, assume a visible and tangible form; and are delineated to the young mind, with a clearness and vividness which more preceptive methods could never impart. And the picture, still more impressively brings the images of the imagination in connexion with the understanding, and subserves the same important purpose.

Stories and prints, being thus important to the success of infant cultivation, should be selected with much discrimination and care. On the fidelity and beauty of their execution, much of their influence will depend. A pure and simple morality, adapted to the circumstances, apprehensions, and wants of infancy, should pervade them.—In supplying the existing wants in this department of infant literature, the highest intellectual and moral attainments might be usefully employed. The writings of Mrs Barbauld, Mr Day, and Miss Edgeworth, may be mentioned as models for imitation; and without which the library of the infant school would be incomplete. Mrs Crabb's '*Familiar Tales*' is also excellent. The simple and beautiful illustrations of virtue in the parables of the New-Testament, and some portions of the Old, will always interest, and, when presented in language adapted to its apprehensions and tastes, improve and elevate the infant mind. There are few books in our language, so far simplified in thought, subject, and expression, that under the perusal of the teacher, further explanation will not be required: and the teacher will always bear in mind, that misapprehension on the part of the child, is perversion and error, of which he is chiefly the cause.

There is no class of writing more happy in its influence upon children, than that which embodies the lives of children. Well written biography carries with it to the young mind, the simplicity and the force of truth and certainty; and conveys instruction in the happiest form. The library of the infant school should contain many books of this character. It is much to be regretted that so few have been written; and that those few have chiefly embodied the lives of children remarkable for some great excellence, or great defect; while the simple, the beautiful, and at the same time, the elevated character of genuine childhood, has been left almost entirely untouched. In everything presented to the infant mind, the true proportions of character should be preserved, and constitute the moral. To make distorted virtue, influence happily the young mind, is both difficult and dangerous. In the story, and in biography, both real and ideal beings are introduced, and whenever the romance of admiration is associated with the imperfections of either, both the moral and influence are false. Unless used in the service of truth, the biography and the tale are equally injurious; but thus used, they become its happiest auxiliaries.

On the influence of fiction upon the mind in early life, Dugald Stewart makes the following remarks;—'The attention of young persons may be seduced, by well selected works of fiction from the present objects of the senses, and the thoughts accustomed to dwell on the past, the distant and the future; and in the same proportion in which this effect is in any instance accomplished, the man is exalted in the scale of intellectual being. The tale of fiction will probably be soon laid aside with the toys and rattles of infancy; but the habits which it has contributed to fix, and the powers which it has brought into a state of activity, will remain with the possessor permanent and inestimable treasures to the latest hour.' How much then may be done for children, by embodying in the tale, the active manifestations of those purer and nobler attributes of humanity, which do not exist in the best specimens of character around them: thus bringing virtue from the skies, to dwell in their presence.

Of the same interesting and improving nature with pictures and stories, are descriptions and specimens of nature and art. By these the young mind is brought in contact with material nature, and through its natural, and always intelligible language, imbibes the unadulterated truths written upon its pages. It cannot range through its vast departments to behold and define its varied imagery and beauty; selections, therefore, from so inexhaustible a cabinet, presented in the picture, the specimen, and the description, supply this inability, in part, and excite much of the enthusiasm of actual observation. Natural history is of itself a world of instruction to the young, and is always studied by them with avidity and happiness. Accurate representations, by cuts, by simple descriptions, and by anecdotes embodying the character of various animals, insects, & etc., are important in early education. Botanical, and geological specimens may likewise be used to much benefit in giving elementary ideas of the subjects which they illustrate.

Besides specimens of nature and art, a few articles of apparatus for illustrating the few principles of science attempted in the infant school, can be used to advantage. Of these, the numeral frame, and a few cubes for illustrating the elements of numbers, manuscript and Roman letters, slates and pencils, black boards, are the chief. An addition of pictures representing scenes in history, of the arts, of life, manners, customs, and natural scenery, might be made of much service. The decoration and internal arrangement of the play-room, and the school-room, might likewise be made to exert a happy and improving influence upon the infant imagination and feelings, A few hundred wooden bricks—a few wheelbarrows—and other articles of amusement in the play-room might also be added.

In applying the principles and methods of the infant system to the developement and discipline of the intellectual faculties, to the formation of just habits of thought, feeling, and action, and to the inculcation of knowledge, it will be important to keep the varied elements of infant nature distinctly in view, and to adapt instructions to the improvement of each. On the ability with which this is done, the harmony and perfection of future character chiefly depends.

Provision is made for the general culture of the animal faculties in the amusements and exercises of the play-room. The eye, the hand, the ear, and the voice, become, however, the subjects of discipline in the school-room. Exercises, among others, favorable for the cultivation of the eye, and hand, are writing and drawing—or what might be more simply expressed, perhaps, by the term, marking. On the slates and black board, the children may delineate in the Roman character, letters, figures, lessons in spelling, in defining, and in arithmetic. In these exercises, both the hand and the eye become associated with the operations of the mind, giving the mechanical facility to the one, and the elementary notions of form and connexion to the other, that will essentially aid the child in his more advanced stages of penmanship. Of himself, he will gradually supply the manuscript character in the expressing of his lessons, and ultimately attain that original style of penmanship suited to his taste and genius, without much formal assistance. And the task of transferring his efforts from the slate to paper, will become comparatively slight. Children are fond of using the pencil and the chalk, and this fondness applied in the exercises of the school, may be made a ready and happy means of employment, and at the same time, prepare them for the more systematic applications of the hand and eye in coming years. An ingenious teacher will not fail of adding a variety of exercises of this nature, to those here mentioned.

In the cultivation of the ear and the voice, vocal and instrumental music, reading, and pronunciation, will form favorable exercises. The instrumental music may be confined to the teacher. Singing is always delightful to children; and the infant school offers a happy means for its attainment. As a moral influence its effect is always happy. How many a rising passion, an unhappy association, may be modified by its influence. In connexion with music, the exercise of marching and the simultaneous movements of the hand accompanying the general exercises of the school, conduce to the improvement of the ear.

Occasions might sometimes, perhaps, occur, when systematic amusements, in the play-room for the discipline of the senses, might be agreeable to the children. Liberty and happiness are, however, so intimately associated in the infant mind, that the interference, would be as unwise as unwished for. *Let us alone in our amusements*, is the true instinct of childhood: and a wise instructer, while he provides careful superintendence, and removes the causes of obvious danger and perversion, will yield obedience to the dictate.

To awaken and to elevate the nobler affections and pure sympathies of infancy, and to check and give habits of self-control to the passions, is an interesting and important feature of the infant system. It is on the state of the affections and passions that infant happiness chiefly depends. The issues of life should, therefore, be guarded with unremitted diligence and care; and the infant heart enshrine in its temple, the objects alone worthy its devotion and its love.

The methods by which these results are chiefly to be produced are involved in the very character of the teacher. From this, and its consequent influence in the discipline and internal management of the school, must they be chiefly anticipated. Sympathy and imitation, adaptation to surrounding influences, are prominent tendencies of the infant mind. Whatever the character of these, such will that of the children insensibly become; and on the teacher the chief responsibility rests. Kindness and affection must form a primary element of his character. It is these which will awaken kindred emotions in the children, and become the chief power of his influence. 'Love and love only' can be with him 'the loan for love.' Cheerfulness, complacency, hope and happiness, dwelling in his bosom, will find way, and, in time, take residence in theirs. By the expression of these, in conversation, by voice, manner, countenance; by frequent appeals to the best affections, drawn from the lessons and incidents of the school-room, from stories, and descriptions, without exciting the passions, the teacher will awaken and purify the infant faculties, and form those habits and dispositions, which prepare the heart for the reception of virtue and happiness. The affectionate nature, thus kept in a state of activity, becomes invigorated, elevated, and improved.

The methods for the developement and illumination of conscience, like those for the cultivation of the affections, are chiefly involved in the character of the teacher. Of all principles of infant nature, the conscience demands the most careful cultivation. On this rest the strong foundations of character: from this come the moral habits of truth, ingenuousness, obedience, approbation, confidence, forbearance, fortitude, justice, generosity, and all those attributes of character, which spread themselves throughout the relations of society and of duty. To awaken and moralise these is an important portion of the teacher's labors. Neglect here, is perversion of all the other powers; for however cultivated the affections and the intellect may be, the want of moral principle, of an awakened and intelligent conscience, will distort the symmetry, and dim the perfections of the soul.

In all things the teacher should strive to be, what to the apprehension of the children, they ought to become. By the kindness of his manner; his love of truth and right above all things; by his obedience to the rules of action which he presents; by appeals to the dictates of conscience, principle, and revelation; by patient, constant forbearance; by the desire in all things to improve and bless; by illustrations of virtue, in stories, in pictures, in descriptions; by remarks on infant character, motives, habits, the teacher will endeavor to reach their minds, impress duty on their conscience, and lead them to its practice. No incident of the play-room, or the school-room, from which profitable instruction can be drawn, will he suffer to pass unused: improvement will come from every influence. What the children thus see the teacher show love and respect for, and to feel an interest in, they will, in time, come to love and respect, and be interested in themselves. The reflection of his character will open the deeper fountains of their nature, and prepare them for the knowledge of themselves. Taught to look within for the dictates of duty, they will be led to the exercise of self-knowledge, and of self-control—the safeguards of virtue and happiness.

The prevalence of the kind affections, the absence of irritating circumstances, combining with the illuminations of conscience, and the aids of self-knowledge and of self-control, render the government of the infant school, exceedingly simple and unimposing. The preventive influences which are thus kept in action, place correction and punishment mostly out of sight. The infant mind is sustained in its progressive course chiefly from within itself; here it finds its impulses to duty, and progress; or when these become powerless or erroneous, the direct influence of the teacher's voice, presence, and character, prevents frequent transgression: the voice of conscience is heard and obeyed. Few laws are, therefore, required, and few punishments and rewards. The child becomes a law to himself.

Sympathy and imitation, the moral action of the teacher upon the children, of the children on him, and on each other, form the common government of the school, and the chief agents of coercive discipline. The teacher cooperates with the children in creating and in diffusing throughout the internal arrangements and exercises of the school, those principles of order and of right, of which all feel the propriety and the need. Of the common conscience of the school, which is thus brought in action, he forms but a part; and it is only when the dictates of this, are inoperative or erroneous, that his personal authority is recognised by the children. Harshness and restraint, fear, and interdiction, arbitrary reward and punishment, where the laws of affection, order, and conscience, generally prevail, will not be often required. The formalities of government may be mostly dispensed with.

To all that affects motive, the teacher will pay particular attention. It is not what hurries the infant mind along the path of knowledge alone with the greatest celerity, that claims so much his attention, as the impulse which prompts, and the means which direct its activity. In operating upon it, therefore, the teacher will be careful in the selection of his means. He will not impair its perceptions of virtue, by too frequently associating with it arbitrary rewards; nor degrade its nature, by recurring too often to arbitrary punishments. These are but the associated supports of the erring and the weak; and a system of government founded chiefly, on these, must of necessity, create the very error and weakness, which it aims to correct. It is only the 'pure in heart that shall see God;' and the infant mind, of all others, should early receive, and act from this impression.

All the essential forms of influencing infancy are expressed and defined, in their purest characteristics, in the nursery. This is the Infant School instituted by creating Wisdom; and all its original relations should be preserved in its extension to numbers, and to the details of their systematic discipline. A faithful observer will not, therefore, defeat his purpose by an essential departure from its requisitions. In its benign and unobtrusive operations, he will recognise its power; and to these will he lend his cooperation and confidence. Familiar and affectionate conversation will become the medium through which he will diffuse his instructions. Encouragement, and approbation, not emulation and reproach, will be made the happiest impulses to duty and progress.

By methods equally simple and maternal, should the intellectual faculties of infancy be addressed. The mere communication of knowledge, though an important, is, by no means, the essential purpose of infant discipline. This is chiefly, the awakening and exciting the mind; the formation of its habits; the preliminary discipline of its faculties for the independent search and acquisition of truth. What, therefore, is presented, refers to its prospective as well as present good; and to accomplish its purpose, must reach the mind, become the subject of its action, and incorporate itself with all its thoughts and habits. Mechanical recitations, wordy lessons, dissociated from the intellect, are to be wholly avoided. That only is worthy of the infant mind, which it can understand and feel. Nature has associated interest, pleasure, and progress, with perception alone; and from mystery and error, the infant mind, of all others, should be scrupulously kept free.

The intellectual faculties, which, among others, should become subjects of cultivation in the school-room, are imagination, association, attention, taste, memory, judgment, reflection, and reason. Of these, the imagination, in infancy, should receive special attention, since, before the dawning of reason, and the exercise of reflection, in connexion with the affections, infant happiness depends much upon its activity and guidance. Early associations of ideas and affections, link themselves so vividly with the prevailing habits of infant thought and feeling, and affect so powerfully and permanently the character of children, that the benevolent teacher will guard this avenue to their minds with the nicest care. The amusements, the government, the stories, the pictures, poetry, and descriptions which he employs for the cultivation and guidance of the imagination, will be selected with the discrimination which belongs to their important influence. They will be accurate representations of the transactions, objects, and duties of coming years. Natural and moral taste will be chiefly dependent on these, for their developement and purity.

In the more individual exercises of the school-room, for the cultivation of memory, judgment, reason, and reflection, the elements of the simplest sciences, and arts, may be happily applied. Attempts, however, should not be made to compel, for any length of time, a strictly scientific application. This is opposed to the prevailing habits of the infant mind. A few elementary facts, spread through the lessons of the school, and wrought up with incident and affection, is all that should be attempted in the way of formal tuition.

Enunciation, spelling the simplest names of familiar objects, actions, and qualities, defining their thoughts, writing, the elements of morality, and natural history, may constitute the chief portion of the children's lessons. During the intervals of more direct influence from the teacher, they may delineate their lessons on the slate and black board. When once interested in the employment of their hands in this way, an ingenious teacher will find in this, an unfailing means of employing their minds. In the succession of their lessons, due reference should be had to contrast and variety. Employment is the great safeguard to infant improvement and happiness; and the attempt to associate this with what is unintelligible to the child, should of all things be avoided. During the early years of infancy, we must be satisfied with making desultory impressions upon the mind; the conclusions of science belong to maturer years.

In the views of infant nature and instruction which have been presented, it has been a primary object to designate those faculties, which from their early prominence, seem designed as subjects of early culture; to present the principles by which these faculties may be effectually addressed and improved; to guard the happiness and true progress of infancy from formal and unintelligible influences; and to lead to the perception of the great and noble objects which infant education contemplates—the formation of a pure, and happy, and elevated character.

These views, principles, and objects, appreciated, and felt, by an intelligent and devoted teacher, may direct and assist him in his work. To him their practical application to the details of the school-room must be chiefly left. His acquaintance with the infant mind; his interest in its progress and happiness, will guide him to the best methods. By him no system will be strictly imitated; but from all systems, he will draw instructions to aid him in the course best suited to his circumstances and location. He who cannot do this, is engaged in a work for which he is unfitted, and his influence must be ineffectual and unhappy. The formation of infant character is a work too great to be entrusted to hands unwise and unskilful. He who operates upon it from imitation alone, has imbibed neither the true spirit of duty nor of success; he can do little for its improvement and happiness. He who has low and imperfect views of the infant mind, cannot fail to pervert and degrade its nature; and of all others will be slow, in forming the conclusion, that '*infant education when adapted to the human being, is founded on the great principle, that every infant is already in possession of the faculties and apparatus required for his instruction, and, that, by a law of his constitution, he uses these to a great extent himself; that the office of instruction is chiefly to facilitate this process, and to accompany the child in his progress, rather than to drive or even to lead him.*'

ADDRESS

ON

INFANT SCHOOLS;

delivered at the request

OF THE

MANAGERS OF THE INFANT SCHOOL SOCIETY.

by William Russell.

Boston:

Hiram Tupper, Printer—School Street. 1829.

ADDRESS

Infant schools are an institution of recent origin; and, in this country, particularly, it is but a short time since they became objects of general attention. Few of our community have had opportunity of personally observing the operation of these schools; and many have necessarily derived all their knowledge of them from occasional report. A brief account, therefore, of the character and design of schools of this description, may not be uninteresting as an introduction to more general statements relating to the same subject.

An infant school may be best described, perhaps, as something which resembles, not so much a school, as a large nursery, and the object of which is to provide for its little inmates employment and amusement, not less than instruction. A number of young children, varying, in different instances, from fifty to one or even two hundred in amount, and embracing all diversities of age, from that of about six years down to that of eighteen months, are assembled to spend the day under the care of a teacher, furnished with the requisite aid of one or more female assistants.

The arrangements made for the benefit of these infant pupils, are designed, in the first place, with reference to *comfort and health*. A spacious, airy, and well lighted room, with several smaller apartments adjoining, as well as a suitable play ground, is accordingly provided in all cases where such advantages are accessible; and the children receive every attention for convenience and health, for their noon meal, for intervals of play, of rest, and even of sleep, which could be devised by the most solicitous care of a mother. In many instances, also, the additional aids of simple taste and decoration have been employed; and the mind of childhood, is delighted with specimens or representations drawn from the vast stores of grandeur and beauty, amid which it is the common privilege of man to be placed by creative Wisdom.

The *intellectual* instruction imparted at these schools, is restricted to a few simple but useful and interesting elements. It embraces the rudiments of arithmetic, a good degree of progress in reading and orthography, some information about animals, plants, and minerals, and the various substances composing articles of daily use in household affairs or the arts of life,—beside other things which it would consume too much time to enumerate.

But the peculiar feature in the infant school system, is, the excellence of its moral instruction, by which the pupils, instead of being made passive recipients of injunctions and silent listeners to truth, are allowed a free and varied intercourse with each other and with their teacher, and are made active and spontaneous agents in their own improvement. The moral lessons of the infant schools, if they ever can be detached from the other departments of instruction and exercise, may be briefly said to resemble, as nearly as possible, the tender, affectionate, and judicious management of a well regulated nursery. In its connexion, however, with the cheering and enlivening influence of numbers, its free scope for social amusement and recreation, and its frequent recourse to the elementary principles of interesting and useful knowledge, the infant school method has some points of superiority over perhaps the best forms of domestic nursery discipline,—for at least that part of the day, which it is desirable to have occupied with instruction.

The moral part of infant school education is eminently *rational* and *affectionate*. It is founded on familiar and common occurrences in the school room,—not conveyed in language always formal and seldom intelligible: it is addressed to the better feelings of the heart, and is communicated in the accents of mild and kind affection: it is elicited from the mind itself,—not forced into it: the little community in the school room is, in fact, converted by skilful cultivation into a vigilant and most efficient society for the suppression of vice. This system throws away entirely the restraints of fear, and substitutes an intelligent and voluntary respect for those moral principles, which, to the unperverted mind of childhood, are intuitive.

To render this general description intelligible to persons who are unacquainted with the particular forms of discipline and instruction adopted in the infant schools, it may be sufficient to say, that the effects mentioned are produced by the personal influence of the teacher himself. He depends for his results chiefly on sympathy and imitation, those powerful principles of action in the young mind: he wishes the children to be uniformly cheerful,—to attain this end, he is so himself: he inculcates tenderness by the mildness of his own manner, and the gentleness of his own tones: he wishes his little pupils to be cleanly and neat in their personal appearance and habits,—he sets them a constant example, and preserves a corresponding effect in the school room and its furniture. He cultivates the sensibility to natural beauty and innocent pleasures by the interest he takes in the play ground and garden, and the care he bestows on them. For rules and penalties he substitutes encouragement and persuasion, and for tangible rewards he uses words and looks of approbation. If one of his little flock become wayward and refractory, instead of attempting to wrench the will from its course by violence, he mildly leads the offender to a group of his fellows who are pleased and busy with their lesson, and leaves him to the restoring influence of their society, and the susceptible spirit within his own little breast. Nature does its genial work; the turbid mind soon becomes serene; reason returns to her supremacy over the soul, bringing back with her the mood of gentleness and love. The softened transgressor returns with a new docility to the performance of his duty.

Those who are familiar with the history of education will recognize the methods adopted in infant schools as embodying the spirit of the system of Pestalozzi,—the greatest benefactor of our age, the truest observer of the human mind, and, (with one sacred exception,) perhaps its benignest friend: the man who was the first to maintain in relation to instruction, and to prove by triumphant experiment, that there is within the human soul that, which to strengthen and expand and cherish and direct, is the sole business of education; that every infant bosom is a mine of unexplored treasure, which cultivation only brings to light; that every child possesses in miniature the attributes of the great Father of spirits; and that in prosecuting moral education, the instructer has only to develope these traits of resemblance. The intellect, he thought, was to become a throne on which the better propensities might sit in perpetual dominion; prostrating and exterminating every passion which is an enemy to the nobler nature, till the great fabric of character rises in the glory of complete and permanent proportion.

It can never be too deeply regretted that this illustrious philanthropist should have been so long misunderstood and misrepresented; and that it was not till towards the close of his invaluable life that the generality, even of intelligent teachers, in this country or in England, recognized his high attributes of professional superiority, the sublimity of his benevolence, the profoundness of his philosophy, and the depth and extent of his experience. The glory of original and beneficent greatness, however, will dwell upon his name, as it descends to distant ages; and history will revert to it with a grateful eye, when numbering the individuals whose minds have impelled the great tide of human improvement.

The children of the present generation are, in most countries of Europe, tracing the path of elementary knowledge under the guidance of his intellect, as communicated in his system of instruction; and the village school boy in New-England finds with equal wonder and delight, that arithmetic, as taught on his principles, is a rational science, founded in his own mind, and assimilated to it.

The system of instruction adopted in the infant schools, is chiefly, then, a transcript of the method of Pestalozzi, applied to the earliest stages of education. It was first introduced into England about nine or ten years ago, by one of those active philanthropists whose names reflect a true splendour on that country. The first attempt to establish a school for infants, (if the information received at this distance is correct,) was made in the metropolis under the domestic roof of that individual; and was thence extended as benevolent persons of influence became acquainted with its character and design, and teachers were prepared, by observing the original model.

With the modesty peculiar to simple motives and pure benevolence, the man to whose efforts society is indebted for the establishment of infant schools, has been so little anxious to assert his claim to public gratitude, that in bringing forward on this occasion the name of Wilson, as that of the founder of infant schools, it must be done as a thing which is gathered by inference from current information, rather than received on any particular authority. Nor is it important in a subject identified as this is with the interests of society, and receiving a fresh impulse from every mind which is applied to it, that we be exact in attempting to assign the merits or the names of individuals. Be he who he may, whose energies were first put forth to devise and to propel this engine of improvement, he carries within his own breast a consciousness for which dominion would be a poor exchange. If he is among those whose daily pursuits merge them in the mass of population congregated in London—'that mighty heart,' which has sent forth some of the noblest impulses of humanity—he enjoys daily the sublime satisfaction of contemplating the fruits of his labours, in the hundreds of fellow beings whom his humanity has been a chief instrument in wresting from the early dominion of ignorance and vice, and raising to the eminence, the purity, and the conscious freedom of intelligence and religious principle. If there is on earth such a thing as the reward of active virtue, it is realized in the soul of that man, as he passes the infant groups repairing to school, whose minds he has rescued from neglect and ruin—whose clean apparel and healthful air of innocent happiness, tell what it is to be redeemed from the influences of domestic misery, and an education in the streets. If he occasionally visits the other cities of his native country, and witnesses the extension and rapid increase of the infant schools, and sees them becoming the elementary part of that system of general education which is now diffusing itself in every part of Britain, and shedding the light of intelligence and of piety over all classes of the people—he perceives that the humble endeavours of an individual, begun and carried on with the sole aid of a good purpose, may do more for human happiness than was ever effected by the enactments of legislators.

Infant schools, soon after their establishment in England, received the aid and the countenance of all classes of the community; and among the friends of the institution were early ranked some of the most eminent and efficient promoters of popular improvement. Under such auspices the number of these schools was rapidly increased, till one or more were established in every considerable town. A highly respectable and influential society has, within a few years, been instituted for the purpose of giving unity, extent, and permanency to the efforts of philanthropy in this interesting sphere of operation. Under the patronage of this society, Mr. Wilderspin, an early and zealous advocate of infant schools, and for some time the superintendent of the one situated in Spitalfields, has been of late employed in visiting the cities and larger towns in the vicinity with the purpose of establishing schools in which his tenants are taught. Consequently, according to the most recent accounts received from Mr. Wilderspin, the result is the achievement of the object.

Whether such schools were needed in the United States, was at one time a question with many; as there was an apprehension entertained, that by rendering the advantages of early instruction too easily accessible, or by offering them, instead of leaving them to be desired and sought for, parents might be rendered indifferent to their responsibilities, and slack in their exertions for their children. Some apprehended, also, that infant schools, having been originally intended for the benefit of that class of society whose daily and hourly occupations prevented, to a great degree, the personal discharge of parental duties, could not be productive of good in a community in which, from its peculiar frame of government, it is so emphatically the interest of all that a high degree of personal and domestic virtue should prevail, and therefore that the sense of responsibility connected with the parental relation should be deeply felt. Any means of diminishing this feeling would prove, it was said, an evil to be deprecated rather than an advantage to be desired. Others thought the very principle on which infant schools are founded, a wrong one—the benevolent desire to aid parental instruction and influence; regarding it as doing, in some measure, a violence to nature, to step between the mother and her offspring, even for the purpose of assisting her.

These objections, it is believed, have been all refuted by the establishment and the actual operation of infant schools on this side of the Atlantic. It is found that, on examination, there are, in all the cities and large towns of the United States, a very numerous class of the population—chiefly, however, of foreign origin—situated exactly as the corresponding class in England; from many (and some of these culpable) causes, unable to afford the education of their children, or unwilling to be at the expense or the trouble. In these circumstances,—as positive compulsion is out of the question, in regard to the discharge of moral and personal duties,—the alternative is simply that of judicious and friendly impulse to the negligent, or the deplorable evil of a vitiated and degraded populace. On experiment, too, it is found that all the evils of gratuitous education are avoided, by merely reducing the terms of tuition, so as to meet the pecuniary condition of families poor in circumstances, but numerous in children, and by dispensing entirely with wages only in cases of extreme indigence. Very often it happens that in this way parents being enabled to educate their children, are induced to make exertions which they never would have made, had the school fees been left at the usual hopeless distance from the reach of their ability. To the poor, in a word, the establishment of infant schools proves a stimulus to industry, and not as had been fancied, an encouragement to sloth.

Neither is the responsibility of the parent in regard to the moral instruction of the child found to be diminished. Infant schools have, after fair experiment, proved themselves an effective aid to parental management,—increasing the moral sensibility of the child,—awakening the parent to new views and more constant exertion. Intelligence enters the poor man's dwelling in the person of his own child, and brings docility, and peace, and happiness along with it. True, it gives the young child an acute sensibility to the faults and the vices of its parent, (if any such exist,) but it is equally true, that, in well authenticated instances, the obdurate heart of a vicious parent has been touched by the innocence of his child, or pierced by an unexpected word of gentle admonition, such as the infant moralist had been accustomed to give or receive, when among his little school fellows. Mothers, too, have thus been restored to conscience and to peace; and wives have acknowledged with tears of joy the reformation of their husbands, and the happiness which had come to dwell within their homes.

It is scarcely necessary to say that the objection against infant schools, which was founded on their interference with parental duty, has proved imaginary. The infant school is found to be a poor mother's best friend; relieving her, during a great part of the day, of the care of that member of her family which is the most difficult for her to superintend and manage—the one between the youngest infant, (which with the household cares is sufficient charge, even to an able body and an active mind,) and the child who is old enough to go to a primary school. A sister is, by this means, often released from premature domestic care, and left free to attend school, for her own improvement. The whole question now touched upon, with all its supposed difficulties, resolves itself into this shape,— Whether it is well to send young children to school a year or two earlier than has been customary, and to allow them the benefit of protection, care, and instruction, adapted to their tender age? This question is fully settled by the effects already attending the infant schools. It is found that infants may not only be kept out of harm's way, and kindly tended, but that they may be kept constantly happy, and be actually taught much that is immediately useful to them as moral beings, and that serves to prepare the way for further instruction in other schools. Mind and body are both turned to good account; both are employed in useful and pleasing ways; both are gently treated and skilfully cultivated. In addition to this, the disposition is developed, and trained to rectitude and happiness; and reason, in all its benignant influence, is brought out to mould the forming character. Let an observer look into one of our infant schools, and he will see a little community unperverted in understanding, fresh and uncontaminated in feeling, prompt and cheerful in action; kindness and joy pervading the whole in common sympathy; actions instantly approved or condemned; all the natural and sinless propensities of animal and intellectual nature in free exercise; admonition given in tones of constant gentleness; instruction expanding and delighting, (never oppressing or straining,) the mind; the whole soul, the whole being, not only unrestrained by arbitrary rule, not only permitted to act, but invited to act, and kept in agreeable action, unless when purposely permitted to rest. No parent, it is believed, has ever left such a scene, without wishing that all classes of society were furnished with such schools, adapted to their condition and brought to their doors.[1]*

To enter into a detailed account of the exact number of infant schools, or of the children estimated to be benefitted by them, would occupy time which perhaps would be more usefully employed in general views of the whole subject, as a department of education, and as a source of valuable instruction to teachers and parents. It must suffice, therefore, for the present, to say that the infant schools, as they exist in England are doing extensive good, by suiting the purpose of preparatory training for the National Schools, or those of the British and Foreign School Society,—a class of schools corresponding in some respects to the common or district schools of New-England. Children are admitted into the infant schools at any age, from that of six years to that of eighteen months; and remain till they are transferred to the other schools mentioned, which they enter at the age of seven years.

---

1. Private schools for infant children, we are happy to observe, are now established; and several are proposed in different vicinities within the city.

In our own country, schools for infants are beginning to be established, or are already in progress, in most of the cities and large towns, and are contributing effectually to the extensive dissemination of instruction and its invaluable benefits. The teachers and patrons of these schools find in them and in the families connected with them, a peculiar and most interesting field for philanthropic exertions. Were it proper to bring before a public assembly the private scenes of beneficence and gratitude, a sufficiency of anecdote could be furnished from the schools in this city, to satisfy the most exorbitant taste. For the present we confine ourselves to the statement of the fact, that these schools are highly useful in conveying a desire for intelligence and a sense of character into families, in which, previously, they were too little felt; and are thus accomplishing their part in the melioration of society.

The early age at which children are admitted to the primary schools of New-England, and those of this city in particular, which receive children at the age of four years, seemed to some persons to supersede the necessity of infant schools, or in fact to preclude their existence entirely. This objection to these schools, has, like all the others made on presumption, been set aside by experience.

The age from two to four years, is precisely that at which a child, whose mother is necessarily much occupied otherwise, is most exposed to danger, and most apt to commit petty faults. It is at this age that the mother most needs assistance in the charge of her offspring, and is consequently, though reluctantly, compelled to resort to the aid of an elder sister or brother, who must be detained from school for the purpose. It is at this age, too, perhaps an attentive observer of the circumstances of the poor would say, that the disposition receives that tinge of bitterness, which so extensively pervades the domestic temper and manners of the poorest class. The innocent little being who is so often thwarted in his wishes, and checked in his actions, and punished for unintentional transgressions, finds himself governed by a capricious and unintelligible authority. He sympathizes of necessity with the angry feeling of which he has been the temporary cause; and he suffers in reality from the pain inflicted on him. By imitative instinct, he treats others as he is treated himself; and long before he is old enough to become a candidate for admission to a primary school, selfishness, in the form of violence and ill temper, has got possession of his heart; and the primary teacher must be efficient indeed, who succeeds in eradicating these. This is no picture of fancy. But assertion is needless to those who have been observers of these things; and to others nothing but observation can carry full intelligence or conviction.

The *intellectual* not less than the moral interests of the rising generation plead for the introduction or the farther extension of infant schools. Along with all due care and protection, much actual instruction may be afforded to infancy; or rather the mind may be early set going in those directions in which it is to move, when the period of education has formally commenced.

The infant stage of life may be seized as a happy opportunity for giving the mind a delight in natural objects and in useful knowledge; for expanding it to the grateful rays of intellectual light, by a wise guidance of the warmth of the heart; for making the young pupil an intelligent and exact observer of facts, an early disciple of nature and its sublime truths. If the little innocent is, according to the irrational though time-hallowed course, to be fastened down, at the age of four, to eight inches of space on a bench, and to the unnatural task of conning the arbitrary marks which are the representatives of speech; if he is to be punished for attempting to change his irksome position; if he is to be taught that it is a crime to smile, and an unpardonable offence to express his thoughts;—let at least two years of his life be spent in freedom and happiness: give him so much time in which to think and act and move as a free agent. Do not begrudge him this season of natural and strong delight in animals and pictures, and new things and new thoughts. Do not hinder him from acting out his impulses and enjoying his nature; for even thus his mind will have been so enlivened and strengthened, that he will prove, at the appointed time, more than a match for the stillest and the tamest pupil of a dull and mechanical discipline. But if all this is not to happen;—if, as is every day taking place, a clearer light is falling on the subject of early education, and our methods of attempting to gain access to the mind are becoming more congenial, more intellectual, more gentle, more cheerful; if the school room is not to be a place of bondage to body and mind; if amusement and recreation are admitted within doors as well as without, and are blended with the exercises of intellect, and the whole course of instruction is 'to pay homage to the mind and its Author;' then by all means embrace these early and precious moments, in which to begin this benign course of development and conscious progress. The good work cannot be commenced too early, if commenced aright. The first indications of the wants of the mind may be read in the natural actions and looks of infancy. Obey these; and watch them, as they become daily more numerous and varied; comply with all that are harmless; follow this course, with the necessary modifications, through the whole period of education; and there will be produced, what, perhaps, has seldom yet been seen in the world of mind, an undistorted, uninjured, unrepressed, human soul, whose vigour, elasticity, proportion, and grace, are but dimly shadowed in the beautiful perfection of those human forms, which suggested the conceptions of the master pieces of human art.

Again; infant schools are needed on the score of health, not less than of mental improvement. To the children of the poor, home has generally few opportunities to afford for healthful recreation. The common air and light of heaven are often in a great measure denied to infancy in this condition; the unaided vigour of the constitution is left to struggle with hindrances, and not unfrequently sinks under the evils of neglect. Our primary schools seldom offer any salutary counteracting influence to early injuries of this nature: they are too generally situated so as rather to prolong or aggravate them. A change, it is gratifying to observe, is now making, by which, it is to be hoped, spacious and pleasant rooms will be furnished for these schools, and the health and comfort of the teachers and the children secured.[1] But this change, desirable as it is, produces of course no change on the condition of infancy—nothing to counteract the disadvantages of damp, unwholesome, unventilated rooms, at that susceptible period; and it is one great purpose of infant schools to provide airy and comfortable rooms, in which the little pupils may spend most of the day. Were no other good whatever effected by these schools, who can estimate the benefit thus conferred by them on the community?

An important object in immediate connexion with our present subject, is the good effected by infant schools, through their influence on elementary instruction generally, and the useful hints which they offer for the management of primary schools, and even the arrangement of the nursery. Of these highly interesting topics there is now little room to treat; and a few only of the more important can but be briefly mentioned.

---

1. It is proposed that the rooms for primary schools be henceforth provided by the city, and not by the teachers. More suitable apartments will thus be obtained without adding to the expense of supporting these schools, or occassioning loss to those who teach them.

The spirit of the methods adopted in the infant schools would contribute effectually to the improvement of all elementary schools; for these methods are strictly practical.

In conducting the business of education, we are too prone to forget that our influence over the mind is not direct and immediate, and that whatever instruction leaves the mind passive merely, is of no real benefit. All living and expansive action in the mind, proceeds from itself and depends on itself. We may succeed fully in conveying to the understanding a given idea, and the intellect yet receive no benefit from it in relation to the purposes of education. To obtain any substantial benefit from an idea received, the mind must act upon it, must assimilate itself to it, must identify it with itself. The most effectual influence over the mental character, therefore, is that which consists in placing objects so skilfully before the mind of the learner, that he recognizes, by his own perceptive power, their individual and relative character, and acquires his whole knowledge of them by his own activity, and not by becoming the passive object on which the mind of his teacher is to act by inculcation. The same thing is true of memory as of intellect. If we would have any fact remembered, we must show it to the sense or to the mind—if we cannot do this, our next resort should be as vivid a delineation of it as possible, whether the representation be offered in the form of a picture or a written or oral description.[1]

Take, for an illustration, the science of grammar as commonly taught in elementary schools; and we find that these principles, though obvious, or at least readily admitted, are entirely overlooked. The first object with most writers on grammar, even when writing for children, is the perfect exactness of a definition abstractly. Hence the great number of abstract terms in all treatises on grammar. But abstract terms, to the juvenile learner, little accustomed to generalize things, much less thoughts or words, are seldom intelligible; and when these are so, the habits of his mind, running chiefly on particulars, render them of little or no use to him, as means of progress or improvement. Grammar, then, when taught after the manner prescribed in most books on that subject, proves commonly to the young mind a formal, dull, unintelligible, and apparently useless branch of study. It is taught, in a word, too theoretically and too systematically. By generalizing to the utmost extent the language in which we convey instruction, and leaving the pupil as few illustrations as possible, on which his mind may alight and dwell, we flatter ourselves that we are at

---

1. In this view of our subject an additional value is imparted to that excellent institution, the American Lyceum; one of the objects of which is, to render associations for mutual improvement among adults, tributary to the improvement of elementary instruction, by furnishing from these sources the simple apparatus and natural specimens used in teaching the rudiments of science. Infant and primary schools generally will thus, it is expected, be provided with materials for rational, useful, and amusing instruction.

once expanding his intellect and condensing his thoughts, and subjecting his powers to a purely intellectual discipline. But in relation to the actual purposes of life, grammar is a practical and a useful science; and he proves the best grammarian who has carefully observed the greatest number of facts, whether in single words or in phrases. Hence the well known circumstance, that many of the most eminent writers in the English language never studied a page in a book of English grammar; and that not a few knew nothing of what is called the grammar of any language.

This illustration has been used—perhaps at the expense of having been found tedious. It suits, however, as well as any that could be found, the object of expressing the difference between the infant school method, and that which is too prevalent in other schools. In the infant schools, the pupils are made familiar with facts, with objects in nature and art; and they are not required to classify these, till they have become acquainted with their points of resemblance and of difference. The grammatical study of words is but sparingly prescribed, and is never separated from a natural reference to the objects or relations which words represent. The mind is not deadened by receiving knowledge in unmanageable masses, or dissipated by acquiring it through the medium of general terms, or enfeebled by unnatural attempts to imbibe it through the sole channel of memory, or rendered superficial by never applying what is acquired. Every thing submitted to the mind is brought, as far as practicable, within the cognizance of the senses: is offered, if possible, to the imagination and the heart, as well as to the understanding and the memory. As under the genial guidance of nature itself, the whole being, physical as well as mental, is called into action: the body ministers to the mind and the mind to the body. Knowledge is thus made to flow into the opening mind through the appointed avenue of the senses; and no overstraining ambition is permitted to distort the mental habits, by attempting to work upon the intellect directly and exclusively.

A beautiful feature in the infant school system of instruction consists in its bringing forward all the faculties in proportion. On the common plan of education the whole nature lies dormant, and neglected,—with the sole exception of the faculty of memory, and sometimes, incidentally, the understanding. Spelling, reading, arithmetic, grammar, may all be named as examples of this sort of tuition, when they are taught in the common mechanical way. As these branches form nearly the whole routine usually pursued at schools, the young labour, for the most part, under all the disadvantages of a defective and unnatural cultivation; and the mind, unless thrown into very peculiar circumstances in the period subsequent to school days, retains more or less the feebleness and helplessness which such a discipline naturally entails. In some cases, the disproportioned exercise of the memory gives it a morbid excess over the other powers; and in others, nature seems to resent the violence done to it; and the memory, so often and so long strained by application, at last ceases to act with any degree of useful efficiency.

The affections, meanwhile, have become morbid from disuse; and the creative fire of imagination has become dim. Taste, sentiment, character, force of purpose, energy of action, are sacrificed in a blind idolatry to memory: tameness, feebleness, and indolence are entailed on the individual, as his habitual attributes. Add to all this the neglect of the corporeal frame, and perhaps the fatal decline of health; and the picture of prevalent education is complete. Is this description a fiction? Who is there among the most favoured offspring of the system of education hitherto pursued, that can be pronounced free from the evils that have been mentioned? Is there a reflecting man of our day who can say that his education, however ample, how ever splendid, has not proved entirely *disproportioned*?

Now, the method exemplified so beautifully in the infant schools, addresses itself first and chiefly to the physical frame and the senses. Its leading object is the securing of health; its next great purpose, is the cultivation of the heart; and the exercise of the intellect is comparatively incidental. But this arrangement, so far from injuring the mind by neglect, only serves to inspire it with a healthy and natural vigour, which carries it onward in the career of improvement, with a velocity and a force never attained by the common methods of instruction and discipline. The human being is advanced as a living whole, and not in dissected and irregular portions.

The method of the infant schools is further recommended by the natural and gradual progress by which it leads the mind onward. The child's attention is turned first to surrounding objects, and not to books and lessons: nature, in its exhaustless variety and beauty, is laid open to his mind. Nothing is forced upon him; and his advance is never hurried. By a gentle and silent guidance, adapted to the tenderness of his age, he is conducted from the observation of things to that of their relations, thence to the tracing of thoughts, and thence to the study of language. All his movements are those of intelligence and gratification. How different and how unnatural the course usually pursued is, it is scarcely necessary to say; violence, to a greater or less extent, being done to the mind, from the very commencement of its discipline, which consists in attempting to discriminate the confused and complicated characters used in the expression of thought.

The infant school methods are characterized by the cheerfulness of their aspect: they abound in amusement and recreation. Intellectual action thus becomes a spontaneous and pleasurable excitement; as it would always be if rightly managed. The incessant alternation of activity and rest, gives no quarter to dullness and absence of mind. The glow of healthful feeling gives a force and buoyancy to the thoughts as well as to the bodily movements; and this is no mean step towards habitual mental energy and moral courage.

On the prevailing plan of education, no definite time is assigned to mental recreation: it is left to be stolen, perhaps, from the hours of sober duty. The propensity to the indulgence of playfulness which seems implanted as a safeguard in every constitution, is quelled by the frown of authority, till the spiritless and exhausted mind yields itself to morbid lethargy and that quiescent inanition, which so often secure, at a cheap rate, the credit of gravity and wisdom. The necessity of corporeal recreation is freely admitted by every body; but the advantage of mental relaxation is seldom adverted to. The professional man understands that if he would preserve his health he must ride or walk; that he must refresh his eyes with the sunlight, and recruit his lungs with the invigorating air, and allow his limbs the privilege of motion. But propose to the same man the equally urgent necessity that his mind should be permitted to reinvigorate itself at the fountains of nature, or recreate itself among the beauties of art, or enjoy the delight of mingling in pleasurable sympathy with the thoughts and feelings of others, or rise for a time on the wing of poetry, or float on the stream of fiction, or watch the gleaming of wit and the play of humour—Speak of all this as essential to the full development and enjoyment of his nature, and therefore to the power of his mind, and the perfection of his character; and you are not understood: at all events you are not listened to, or you are declared extravagant.

A close observer, however, of human nature might trace in the occasional depression or flatness of the mind, and the wandering of thought, which are so often complained of, by all men, the want of a healthful and inspiring mental regimen. In gayer communities than that of New-England, these things are better understood, and in some which are quite as grave, but perhaps more judiciously considerate of the human constitution.

In following these thoughts I have not left the subject of infant schools; for it is among their many recommendations that they multiply the innocent pleasures of childhood, and impart a cheerful tone of mind, which naturally becomes the habit of after life; that they anticipate and remove evils which too often arise from neglecting the natural propensities of the mind and the enjoyment of those intervals of healthful relaxation, which give elasticity to the spirit, and prepare it for vigorous, efficient, and useful activity.

Made in the USA
Middletown, DE
13 June 2017